The Golf Joke Book

The Golf Joke Book

Bob Lonigan

BARNES
&NOBLE
BOOKS
NEW YORK

1996 Barnes & Noble Books

Design and typography by Noble Desktop Publishers

Cover cartoon by Bill Woodman

ISBN 0-7607-0032-X *casebound*
ISBN 0-7607-1526-2 *paperback*

Printed and bound in the United States of America

99 00 01 02 MC 9
99 00 01 02 03 MP 9 8 7 6 5 4 3 2 1

BVG

For helping me with the jokes, cartoons, quotes, stories, and advice on my golf grip, I want to thank a number of people including Orlando Busino, Jerry Marcus, David Binswanger, Sam Gross, Leo Cullum, Brian Savage, Tim Charlton, Blake Lochrie, Bill Thompson, Bill McIntosh, George Jurlus, Artemis Cole, Bill Maul, Boris Drucker, Frank Hoffman, and Bill Woodman.

Folger was searching through the woods for his lost ball when he stumbled upon another golfer from the adjoining fairway apparently doing the same thing. After the two of them had been poking around in the underbrush for a minute or so, Folger yelled out, "Are you looking for a Wilson?"

"No, I'm looking for a Jasper," the other fellow yelled back.

"Jasper? Is that your ball?"

"Who said anything about a ball?" bellowed the man. "Jasper is my caddy."

It matters not the sacrifice
Which makes the duffer's wife so sore
I am the captain of my slice
I am the servant of my score.

Grantland Rice

Smith complains that he's a two-handicap golfer: his boss won't let him off early, and his wife keeps him home on the weekends.

Juanita returned home with a big smile on her face. Her husband, hard at work in the garden, looked up as she got out of her car. "You're smiling, Juanita. You must have had a great round of golf."

Juanita shook her head. "No. But for the first time I found more balls than I lost."

Glenn, a businessman, was frequently out of the office playing golf. He carefully instructed his assistant to tell anyone who called that he was away from his desk and would get back to them. Then the assistant would call Glenn, who would return the call—from his golf cart.

Tony, Glenn's longtime golf partner, was driving to his match with Glenn when he realized that he didn't know at which of two golf courses they were to meet. Quickly, he called Glenn's office, only to run into Glenn's loyal assistant, who kept repeating that Glenn was away from his desk and would get back to him. Exasperated at the assistant's stonewalling, Tony yelled into the telephone,

"Just tell me, is he ten miles from his desk, or twenty miles?"

"So, son, what are you going to do with your life now that you've graduated from college?" asked Benton.

"I've given it some thought, Dad," replied the young man. "And I've decided to just play golf every day."

"Are you crazy?" shouted Benton. "Do you think I'd allow any son of mine to spend his life running around a golf course?!"

"Of course not, Dad. I was hoping you'd buy me a golf cart."

"Every day they get a new hazard on this course."

It was a beautiful summer morning as Janet and Laura stepped up to the first tee. Laura teed up her ball, then unleashed a long, perfect drive that caught a gust of wind and carried to the green. There it rolled fifty feet and dropped in the cup. Both golfers stared at the distant pin for a moment before Janet spoke. "Nice hit, Laura. Now I'm going to take *my* practice shot."

There are two things that won't last long in the this world, and that's dogs chasing cars and pros putting for pars.

Lee Trevino

Under the watchful eye of the pro, Barbara took out her driver, addressed the ball, and swung. "Any advice?" she asked.

"Well, I think your ball will go further if you take the hood cover off the driver."

Sam and Herman were business partners who competed hard in every aspect of their lives. Especially golf, though they had long ago agreed that the only way the two could play eighteen holes together without killing each other was to never say a word. And so it had been for fifteen holes. The sixteenth hole proved a disaster for Herman after he found his approach shot just off the green. First he lofted a 9-iron from one side over the green to the other. Then he repeated it again, and again. Several times Sam cleared his throat as if to speak, but thought the better of it. When he did it a third time, Herman stopped, turned around, and glared at his partner. "I thought we had an agreement not to say anything on the golf course."

"I know, Herm, but I just wanted to say one thing."

"Yeah, what is it?"

"You've been hitting my ball."

The game of golf was launched at 11:10 a.m., the first lie about a scorecard at 11:22, and the first golf joke at noon.

Bennett Cerf

Charlie came running up just in time to join his companions on the first tee. "Good to see you, Charlie," said one friend. "But since it's Sunday morning, we didn't think you'd be here."

"Yes, it was a toss of the coin between playing golf and going to church."

"So why are you so late?" the friend asked.

"I had to toss the coin fifteen times!"

The young pro had been on the European tour for three months, and the separation from his wife had been difficult for both of them. When he finally returned home the two flung themselves into each other's arms in a passionate embrace. Hours later, the exhausted young couple lay in bed sleeping when all of a sudden there was a loud pounding at the door.

The jet-lagged pro opened one eye and groggily rasped, "It must be your husband."

"Couldn't be," his wife sleepily replied. "He's in Europe playing golf."

Ben, a visiting pro who was staying at a lush Florida resort, was stroking putts on the practice green when he was approached by another golfer who was looking for a partner. After the pro agreed to play, the golfer asked Ben what he shot.

"Oh, around a hundred," said Ben, looking to pick up a little extra cash on his vacation. "Care to wager on the match?"

"Sure," said the golfer. "It sounds like we're about the same."

Ben smiled over to the resort's pro as he and the mark strolled to the first tee.

Three hours later Ben stormed in from the eighteenth hole and ran into the pro from the resort. "How'd you do, Ben?" asked the pro.

"That lying SOB told me he shot 100," snarled Ben. "I had to shoot an 82 just to win the bet!"

Golf is . . .

A game you play with your worst enemy—yourself.

Finley Peter Dunne

The most fun you can have without taking your clothes off.

Chi Chi Rodriguez

A game in which you claim the privileges of age and retain the playthings of youth.

Samuel Johnson

A game that begins with a golf ball and ends with a high ball.

Bert Sugar

A game in which a ball 1 ½ inches in diameter is placed on a ball 8,000 miles in diameter. The object is to hit the small ball but not the larger.

John Cunningham

A game in which the ball lies poorly and the players well.

Art Rosenblum

13

"Becky, if you don't stop nagging me," yelled the golfer to his wife, "you'll drive me out of my mind."

"That wouldn't be a drive," she yelled back. "That's more like a gimme putt!"

"I'm on a golf kick. When he mentions golf, I kick him."

Through years of experience I have found that air offers less resistance than dirt.

Jack Nicklaus

Bart and his wife Sheila were playing a round of golf together when he hooked a drive behind a barn that was next to the fairway. When they found his ball, Sheila pointed out that the doors on both sides of the barn were open. "Why not hit it through the barn?" she suggested.

Bart agreed. He took a mighty swing and struck the ball squarely. Unfortunately, it hit the top of the door and bounced backwards, striking Sheila in the middle of the forehead and killing her instantly.

Several years later, Bart was playing the same course with a friend when he again hooked his shot behind the barn. He started to pick up his ball and take the penalty strokes, but his partner interrupted.

"Wait a minute, Bart. The doors on both sides of the barn are open. Hit an iron shot through and you'll be okay."

Bart sadly shook his head. "No, the last time I tried that I got a triple bogey."

I'm playing like Tarzan—and scoring like Jane.

Chi Chi Rodriguez

The two women golfers were both using Titlist balls. On the ninth hole, they both hit their best drives of the day, and when they reached the middle of the fairway, one ball was sitting up high, while the other was half buried under a stone.

"I'm sure this is my ball," said Wilma, pointing to the ball in the good position.

"No, I'm sure that's my ball," insisted Diane. "Yours is over there under the stone."

The argument got more and more heated until finally they decided to enlist the aid of the club pro to settle the dispute. Several minutes later he strolled over from the pro shop, glanced down at the two balls, and looked at the two women.

"Ladies, I think we can settle this pretty quickly. Which one of you is playing the yellow ball?"

"I'd like to buy two dozen balls and have my name stamped on them," said the golfer in the pro shop.

"No problem, sir."

"Can you also put 'CPA' after my name?"

"Plenty of room for that, sir."

"Then how about adding my telephone, FAX number, and 'hours nine to five every day except Wednesdays!'"

The two women were put together as partners in the club tournament and met on the putting green for the first time.

After introductions, the first golfer asked, "What's your handicap?"

"Oh, I'm a scratch golfer," the other replied.

"Really!" exclaimed the first woman, suitably impressed that she was paired up with her.

"Yes, I write down all my good scores and scratch out all the bad ones!"

Sarah's ball was sitting on the edge of the green, and she decided to bump and run a 5-iron shot. She paced off the distance, wet her finger and held it up to the wind, and cleared away every leaf, stick, and impediment, real and imagined, between the ball and the hole. She carefully felt the grass to see how short it was cut and in what direction. Finally, she took her position only to wiggle and shake for another minute until her partner threw up her hands. "For God's sake, Sarah," she said in exasperation. "Are you gonna take all day?"

Sarah paused and looked over. "My husband is up in the clubhouse watching us, so I want to make sure this shot is a perfect one."

"Forget about it, Sarah. You'll never hit him from here."

When I hit the ball I want somebody else to go chase it.

Baseball player Rogers Hornsby,
on why he didn't play golf

For eighteen holes, Thompson's caddy had been cackling and snickering after every shot that the golfer took. Fed up with the not-so-subtle criticism, Thompson finally threw his putter at the caddy and snapped, "You must be the worst caddy in the world."

The caddy grinned. "That, sir, would be too great a coincidence."

The two men were waiting on the platform for the 8:08 to pull in.

"Haven't seen you at the club, Chad. You still playing golf?"

Chad shook his head. "No, I swore it off. Joined Golfers Anonymous instead."

"What's Golfers Anonymous?"

"Well, whenever you feel the urge to play a round of golf, you call a fellow member and he comes over and drinks with you instead."

You can always spot an employee who's playing golf with his boss. He's the fellow who makes a hole in one and says, "Oops."

Bob Monkhouse

Golf seems to me an arduous way to go for a walk. I prefer to take the dogs out.

Princess Anne

"Caddy, why do you keep looking at your watch?" questioned Harris.

"It's not a watch, Mr. Harris. It's a compass."

"My husband just ran off with my golf partner," lamented Debby.

"It'll be all right," consoled Gilda. "You're a bright, funny, good-looking woman—you'll find another husband."

"It's not that. Where can I find another partner who can play three times a week?"

"It's my ex-husband. Wait till he's at the top of his backswing."

Richard, a novice golfer, showed up for his first lesson with the golf pro at the club.

"I am recently retired," said Richard, "and I've done nothing but work twelve hours a day for seven days a week all my life. Never took a vacation. Now that I'm home all the time, my wife bought me these clubs and says that if I don't take up golf or some hobby she's going to divorce me."

The pro went through the rudiments with Richard and then took him out to the first tee.

"Now what?" asked Richard

"Take out your 1-wood, remember the basics, and hit the ball straight," the pro instructed.

Richard did as he was told and blasted a tee shot straight and far. The pro was too stunned to say anything as they walked down the fairway to the first green. There was Richard's ball not more than three feet from the cup.

"What do I do now?" asked Richard.

"Just putt it into the cup."

Richard slammed down his bag. "Now you tell me!"

Simmons and his caddy were poking through the rough, looking for Simmons's errant shot. From fifty yards ahead Simmons' partner yelled back, "What kind of ball is it?"

The caddy promptly answered, "A brand-new ball, never been properly hit!"

Sam Snead, well known for not suffering fools lightly, was conducting a clinic at a country club. A woman interrupted his talk to ask, "Mr. Snead, how do you make a 3-iron back up?"

Snead looked at her for a moment, then asked, "Ma'am, how far do you hit a 3-iron?"

"About 150 yards," the woman replied.

"Then why in the hell would you want to back it up?" snapped Snead.

Monroe and her caddy were searching for her ball when the caddy pointed to a ball in the rough. "There's your ball, Mrs. Monroe," he said.

"That can't be my ball," protested Monroe. "It looks far too old."

"But, ma'am," the caddy retorted, "it's been a long, long time since we started."

One day a priest was playing an ancient Scottish course and after hooking his tee shot found himself in a deep fairway bunker. His ball was buried in sand at the base of the six-foot-high bunker wall. The priest shook his head, turned his face toward Heaven, and said, "God, please help me." Pausing for a moment to catch his breath he whispered, "And, God, don't send Jesus. This is no shot for a boy!"

Brian met Father Fahey on the church steps after Mass.

"Father, I must ask you something. Sunday is the Lord's day. Is it a sin to play golf today?"

The priest took his arm. "Brian, my boy, I've seen your golf game, and the way you play, it's a sin any day."

I've got to figure out a way to take a vacation from a vacation.

> Dave Stockton, on playing
> the PGA Senior tour

"You never think of me, Ben," wailed his wife. "You are never here. Every Saturday and Sunday you're off playing golf. I'd have a stroke if you ever spent a weekend at home."

"Trying to bribe me, Karen?"

Golferswhotalkfastswingfast.

> Bob Toski

"Harry, you have a great short game," complimented his partner. "Too bad it's off the tee!"

The loudest sound you hear is the guy jangling coins to distract a player he bet against.

Jim Murray

"I just got a new set of golf clubs for my husband," beamed Jane to her golf partner.

"Gee, what a great trade!"

Jeff was by himself at the first tee when another club member introduced himself as Arthur and asked if he could join him. "Sure thing," replied Jeff. Thinking he might wager something, he asked the newcomer what he went around in.

"72," replied Arthur, causing Jeff to reconsider his bet. But as the man began hacking his way along, it quickly became apparent that Arthur's game was something short of scratch.

Then, after putting out on the eleventh hole, Arthur picked his ball up and shook hands with Jeff. "I'm done. I'm heading in for a shower and drink."

Jeff was astonished. "I thought you said you went around the course in 72?" he queried.

"Oh, I do," answered Arthur. "And one of these days I'm gonna actually do it for eighteen holes!"

The IRS has made liars out of more Americans than the game of golf.

Will Rogers

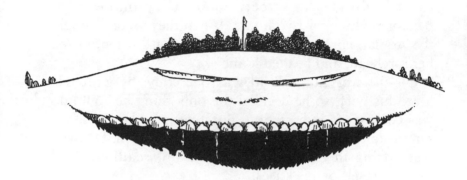

"I always stink on this hole, and I get this feeling that it's mocking me."

After a round of golf, Brad stopped for a beer at a bar a few miles from the golf course. After ordering, he spied a beautiful blond woman a couple of seats away, and since they were both alone, Brad struck up a conversation. One beer led to another, and after several hours, she invited him back to her place conveniently located down the street. There they made mad, passionate love for two hours. When they were through, the woman lay back exhausted. Brad got dressed, kissed her forehead, and headed home.

On the way home Brad was overcome by guilt. He loved his wife, so he decided the only thing he could do was confess his indiscretion. Bursting into the house, he ran upstairs and threw open the bedroom door. His wife was sitting in bed with the lights on, reading. Brad threw himself on his knees.

"Honey, I have a confession to make. After I played golf today, I stopped by a bar for a beer, met this beautiful woman, went back to her place, and made love to her for two hours. But I love you and I won't do it again. Please, say you'll forgive me."

His wife looked up at him and snarled, "Don't try and lie to me, you so and so! You played thirty-six holes, didn't you?"

"Lee, let's stop by the clubhouse and pick up a fifth for golf."

"You mean a fourth."

"No, a fifth. I'm thirsty."

"Very nice clubs, Polly. And brand new."

"Yes, Bill bought them for me."

"Oh, what's the occasion?"

"Nothing. I caught him fooling around with our maid."

"Really! Did you fire her?"

"Of course not," responded Polly. "I need her as much as I need a new set of clubs!"

What I like about golf is that there are no bad calls.

Ivan Lendl

"Say, a box of a dozen Titlists dropped out of my cart on the twelfth fairway," Mack said to the man at the pro shop. "Did anyone turn them in to lost and found?"

"Just the foursome following you."

Beverly and Kimberly had both hooked their tee shots down the left side of the fairway into the rough. Between them and the green was a huge yawning sand trap. Beverly hit a nice 3-iron to the front of the green, but Kimberly topped her shot, and it dropped into a veritable Grand Canyon of a sand trap.

While Beverly putted out, Kimberly disappeared down in the trap. A few minutes later her ball sailed out and plunked on the green, where she then putted out.

"What'd you get, Kimberly?" Beverly asked.

"A six," Kimberly blithely replied.

"Six!?" questioned Beverly. "I distinctly heard you swing at least that many times while you were buried in the sand trap."

"No, I only took three shots down there," Kimberly corrected. "The other three were echoes!"

Just remember. Golf is flog spelled backwards.

Milton Berle

For his regular Sunday morning game Jack showed up followed by two caddies. "How come you brought along two caddies today?" asked one of the other golfers.

"The wife thought I wasn't spending enough time with the kids."

The golfer looked in his bag and pulled out a club.

"You're going to use a 5-iron on this hole?" snorted the caddy. "It's 350 yards!"

The golfer turned to the caddy. "Listen, when I want a surveyor, I'll call you."

28

Golf is . . .

A good walk spoiled.

Mark Twain

A game in which you yell "fore," shoot six, and write down five.

Paul Harvey

The hardest game in the world to play and the easiest to cheat at.

Dave Hill

A compromise between what your ego wants you to do, what experience tells you to do, and what your nerves let you do.

Bruce Crampton

A plague invented by Calvinist Scots to as a punishment for man's sins.

James Reston

A game whose aim is to hit a very small ball into an even smaller hole, with weapons singularly ill designed for that purpose.

Winston Churchill

Sally and Bob met, had a whirlwind courtship, and were soon married. After the reception, they were changing for their honeymoon trip when Bob spoke up. "Sally, I've got a confession to make. It's a lovely, romantic resort we're going to, but the real reason I picked it is for its great golf courses." Bob shook his head. "I am just crazy about golf. I can't get enough of it. I think about it all the time, play it every chance I get. I'm afraid golf is my obsession."

Sally looked at her new husband for a long moment. "As long as we are baring our souls here, Bob, I should be frank with you as well. I'm a hooker."

"That's not a problem, Sally," Bob cried passionately, taking her hands in his. "Just move your left hand higher and hold your club like this."

Find a man with both feet firmly on the ground and you've found a man about to make a difficult putt.

Fletcher Knebel

A salesman was leaving the office for a round of golf when his boss stopped him.

"Harrison, if you spend all your time on the golf course, you won't have anything put aside for a rainy day."

"Of course I will, boss. My desk is piled up with work I've put aside for a rainy day!"

At a cocktail party two women were discussing golf. "So what's your handicap?" asked the first.

"Ten," answered the second.

The first raised her eyebrows in surprise. "Honestly?"

"What's that got to do with it?"

*"He can't answer the phone right now. He's on the fairway.
I mean he's in the hallway."*

I used to play golf with a guy who cheated so badly that he once had a hole in one and wrote down zero on the scorecard.

Bob Bruce

Willie Nelson, discussing what par is on a golf course he bought.

It's anything I want it to be. For instance, the hole right here is 47, and yesterday I birdied the sucker.

At a church social, two women were discussing their respective marriages. "I haven't seen my husband in six years," said the first.

The other looked at her. "Maybe he took up golf!"

The priest eyed his third putt on the green, steadied himself, and stroked the ball. It rolled in a straight line, then curled away from the cup, missing by just a hair.

"Darn," sighed the priest.

"I'm sorry, Father," admonished his partner. "But if you don't learn to swear better, you'll never break par."

The minister happened to overhear a discussion between two boys that consisted mostly of swear words. Leaning out his window, he eyed the two youths. "Do you know what happens to boys who swear all the time?" he asked.

The two stared up mutely.

"They grow up to be golfers!"

"Are you still caddying over at the club, Bob?"

"No, they fired me."

"How come?"

"I couldn't learn to laugh quietly."

The company's most successful salesman was surrounded by his contemporaries at a sales meeting.

"Barry, I don't know how you do it every year," one of them marveled. "You're always the top producer. What's your secret?"

The salesman smiled. "I just follow certain rules. I know my territory, and I know the products. I follow up and I work hard. But when I'm out with my customers there is one rule I follow that I think is the main reason for my success."

The other sales reps leaned forward for the answer.

"I miss my putts by six inches."

"How come you and Roy don't play golf together anymore?" asked Libby of her husband.

"Hah," said Tom dismissively. "Would you want to play golf with a guy who constantly moves his ball to a better position, throws his ball ahead when you're not looking, and shaves strokes when he's keeping score?"

"Certainly not," replied Libby.

"Well, neither does Roy."

Alex and Barney finally finished the eighteenth hole, and Barney was writing down the score as they walked off the green. "What'd you get, Alex?"

"Another twelve. That gives me a 147 for the round."

They had just reached the caddy shack when Alex spoke up again. "What should I leave for the caddy, Barney?"

"How about your clubs!"

Alice teed up another ball and topped it, sending it bouncing down the fairway.

"I keep topping the darn ball," she muttered in exasperation.

Her partner looked over and smiled brightly. "Try teeing the ball upside down."

I'd give up golf if I didn't have so many sweaters.

Bob Hope

Chi Chi Rodriguez, on his accent:

After all these years, it's still embarrassing for me to play on the American golf tour. Like the time I asked my caddie for a sand wedge and he came back ten minutes later with a ham on rye.

The doctor finished up his yearly exam on Blodgett and then gestured for the patient to take a seat. "You've gained forty pounds in the past year, Mr. Blodgett," said the doctor, looking down at his chart. "This is not good for you."

"You're right, doctor," sighed Blodgett. "And it's played hell with my golf game. The balls I can see, I can't reach, and the balls I can reach, I can't see."

A duffer named Kevin was paired with one of the club's good players, and he was anxious to get some free advice. Hitting first, he swung awkwardly and topped his drive. "Do you see anything I can correct?" he asked.

"I see you're standing too close to the ball," the other remarked. "After you hit it."

The foursome was on the fourteenth green, and the last golfer in the group was putting out. Just then, a ball landed on the front of the green, took a bounce, and struck the man in the head. Startled, he dropped his putter, turned, and spotted the culprit who had hit the ball from some 150 yards back on the fairway. Rubbing the back of his head, he ran toward the man.

"You son of a gun, you should have waited till we putted out. I'm going to sue you for $500,000."

The man raised his hands in protest. "I said 'fore.'"

The other man stopped. "I'll take it."

"I don't care if he eagled with a great shot. I'm penalizing him a stroke for excessive celebrating."

"Why yes, Mrs. Feeny. . . . In fact I have your file in front of me right now"

I am not saying my golf game went bad, but if I grew tomatoes they'd come up sliced.

Lee Trevino

It was midmorning on the practice tee, and the club pro was giving instructions to a beginning golfer.

"Let's just go through the motions without actually driving the ball," said the instructor.

"But that's exactly the difficulty I'm trying to overcome!"

The new golfer was on the practice tee with the club pro.

"What's the best way of addressing the ball?" asked the beginner.

"Just include enough information so when you lose it, it'll be returned to you."

The neophyte golfer turned to the caddy on the first tee and asked for his putter. He then drove the ball 280 yards down the middle of the fairway. When he reached the ball, he asked the caddy for his driver and proceeded to knock the ball six inches away from the cup. Next requesting a sand wedge, he popped the ball in the hole for an eagle.

"This looks like trouble," he said, looking in the hole.

"What could be the matter?" asked the astonished caddy.

The golfer pointed down. "What club do I use to get it out of there?"

Bob was just finishing his coffee in the nineteenth-hole restaurant when his friend Tommy came in.

"Man, what took you so long out there?" demanded Tommy. "I thought you and Barbara were going to play a quick round and then you were going to meet me here for lunch?"

"Yeah, I'm sorry," said Tommy, "but on the second hole Barbara had a heart attack and died."

"That's terrible!" gasped Bob. "So what did you do?"

"What could I do? All morning it was hit the ball, drag the body. Hit the ball, drag the body."

Ralph finished pacing off a putt of some thirty feet and stepped up to the ball. "Caddy, is this green watered once or twice a day?"

"Twice, sir."

"And is the green cut from the left or the right?"

"Left, sir."

"And was it cut this morning?"

"Yes, sir."

With that, Ralph finally putted, missing the hole by ten feet.

"Dammit, caddy. What *time* was it cut?"

I don't like to watch golf on television. I can't stand whispering.

David Brenner

Benjamin and Bryant were on the first tee at the Crestwood Club, with Benjamin hitting first. He looked out at the far pin, pulled out his 1-wood, and said confidently, "That's a drive and a putt in my book."

He then took a mighty swing and lifted a long divot, but his ball dribbled only about three feet in front of his tee.

Bryant watched the ball come to a stop before saying anything. "Left yourself one hell of a putt."

I can airmail the golf ball, but sometimes I don't put the right address on it.

Jim Dent

While the choir was singing, the minister looked out over the full pews and then whispered out of the side of his mouth to the deacon.

"You can always tell the golfers in the congregation. When they pray, they use an interlocking grip."

Debby and Emily were sitting in the clubhouse after a round of golf.

"First it was my marriage," said Emily unlacing her shoes. "Now the magic has gone out of my putter!"

A hole in one, scored by accident, can keep a complete duffer playing golf for the rest of his life.

"Champagne" Tony Lema

Two ants were in a sand trap watching a duffer flailing away.

"Quick," said the one ant to the other. "Get on the ball before he kills us."

In 1948, Texan Jimmy Demaret was playing in a match in the U.S. Open in Los Angeles. His approach shot to the green was a bit strong, and as the ball rolled swiftly off the back of the green, the crowd parted politely to allow it to continue to roll. "Damn," said Demaret as he approached the green. "Aren't there any Texans here?"

It was the middle of the week, and Michael and Thos were playing a fast round of golf when they were held up by two women duffers ahead of them.

"Man, look at them hacking away," said Thos disgustedly. "We'll be out here all day. I'm going to go ask them if we can play through." He dropped his golf bag and walked on ahead.

A minute later he was back, ashen-faced. "You know who that is?" he hissed. "It's my wife and my mistress."

"Don't worry. Let me go ask them if we can play through," said Michael, and he set off. But a minute later he too was back.

"Funny coincidence."

"We've been a bit slow. Maybe we should let them play through."

Emily looked at the ball sitting in the rough and asked her caddy for a 5-iron. She took a big swing, and the ball went flying, hit a tree, and bounced back some twenty yards behind her.

"I have never played this badly before," she sighed.

The caddy widened his eyes. "You've played before?"

I'm hitting the woods just great, but I'm having a terrible time getting out of them.

Harry Toscano

Jesus, Moses and an old man were partnered together in the Heavenly Golf Tourney. Moses was the first to tee off. He tucked in his robes, took a tremendous roundhouse swing, and drove his ball straight into a lake that bordered the fairway.

"Oh, a plague upon that ball!" Moses exclaimed. Then he waved his hand, parted the waters of the lake, walked in and retrieved his ball.

Next up was Jesus. He took a perfect swing. The ball flew far and straight down the fairway, took several long bounces, and rolled up the green and into the hole. He nodded his head knowingly and said, "Only because it is the will of my father."

Then it was the old man's turn. He swung as best as he could, only to hook the ball some fifty yards to the left and heading for the lake. But just before it landed in the water, a frog leaped up and caught the ball in its mouth. Then an eagle swooped down, snatched the frog, and flew away. But a hunter with a bow and arrow appeared on the far shore, took aim, and sent an arrow winging at the bird. The arrow (which had a rubber head, of course—this was, after all, Heaven.) struck the eagle between the eyes, stunning him and the frog fell, landing on the green. The ball popped out of the frog's mouth and rolled straight toward the hole, hung on the edge, and fell in for an ace.

Jesus looked over at the old man and muttered disgustingly, "Stop showing off, Dad."

"If you build it they will come."

Steve Gold, a dentist, was leaving the office with his golf clubs slung over his shoulder when his receptionist stopped him.

"It's Mrs. Wall on the phone, Doctor. She wants an appointment this afternoon. What should I tell her?"

"Tell her I can't possibly see her this afternoon. I'm very busy. I've got eighteen cavities to fill."

Bill shook his head as he watched another one of his fairway shots bounce along some fifty yards ahead.

"I'd move heaven and earth," he sighed, "to get a couple of decent shots out here."

"I'd work on heaven," his companion retorted. "You've already moved enough earth."

Marilyn closed her eyes, took a big swing at the ball, and hit a shot that slammed into a tree about twenty yards to the right of the tee and came caroming directly back to her. Instinctively, she dropped her club and caught the ball in her hands. Marilyn then turned to her caddy. "Now what should I do?"

"I'd try the same shot," he replied. "But this time keep your hands in your pockets."

Arnold Palmer is the greatest crowd pleaser since the invention of the portable sanitary facility.

Bob Hope

Jennifer looked at the caddy who had been assigned to her. "How much is four and seven and three, caddy?"

The caddy looked perplexed. "Nine?"

Jennifer smiled. "You'll do just fine."

Man blames fate for other accidents but feels personally responsible for a hole in one.

Martha Beckman

"I tell you, Phil, that's the last time I'm playing golf with Lee," said Tim. "The man cheats."

"How do you know he cheats, Tim?"

"Because he hit a ball that I swear went into the woods. We went looking for it in there, couldn't find it, and then the ball magically appears two feet off the edge of the green."

Lee looked at him. "Well, maybe it bounced off a tree and ended up there. Is that possible?"

"Not likely. I had his ball in my pocket."

The minister and the rabbi were on the fifteenth hole when suddenly the heavens opened up and a torrential thundershower began. The rabbi started to head for the shelter of a towering oak tree on the edge of the fairway when his friend stopped him.

"You can't go there, it's too dangerous. It's the tallest thing around here. If God were to let a lightning bolt hit, it would strike that tree and kill you. And if we stay out here, we might get hit as well."

The rabbi paused momentarily, but then pulled a club out of his bag, held it over his head, and started walking toward the clubhouse.

"What are you doing?" shouted the minister.

"I'm holding up a 1-iron," yelled the rabbi. "Even God can't hit a 1-iron."

Bob and Fred had just finished putting out on the first hole, and Bob had his pencil out to record the score. "What'd you get, Fred?" he asked.

"Six," Fred replied. "And you?"

"Five."

After the second hole, Bob again asked Fred his score.

"Nothin' doing, Bob. It's my turn to ask first."

My best score is 103, but I've only been playing for fifteen years.

Alex Karras

The only thing I fear on a golf course is lightning—and Ben Hogan.

Sam Snead

Jackson was first up in his foursome. Eyeing the ball, he swung his club and hooked his shot over the fence and down a road where the ball crashed through the windshield of an oncoming car. The startled driver lost control of his vehicle, and it spun into a parking lot and bounced off three cars.

Jackson raced over to the crash scene and was relieved to find that no one was hurt. Almost immediately a policeman arrived and spotted Jackson standing next to the crashed car eyeing his ball.

"Just what are you going to do about this?" demanded the policeman.

Jackson looked up. "Well, the first thing I'm going to do is change my grip."

Dick and Todd were putting when a golfer from the foursome behind them came up, followed by a large Great Pyrenees dog with a golf bag strapped on top of him.

Todd looked at the man. "You are one clever golfer," said Todd admiringly.

"He's not so clever," growled the dog. "He still needs me to tell him what club to use."

Sam and Jillian were lying in bed talking.

"I suppose if I died you already have your eye on some pretty young thing to take my place," said Jillian.

"Maybe."

"And I suppose you'd even have her share our bedroom and our bed," snapped Jillian.

"Maybe."

"And I suppose you'd even let her use my golf clubs," sobbed Jillian.

"Nope," muttered Sam. "She's left-handed."

The two duffers cautiously approached the tee and looked out at the green. Between them and the flag was nothing but two hundred yards of water.

"Go ahead, Fred. You hit first."

Fred swung, and his first shot plunked down in the lake. His second shot did no better, and his third splashed down as well.

"You ought to use an old ball on this one, Fred."

Fred looked at his partner. "I've never had an old ball!"

Serenity is knowing that your worst shot is still going to be pretty good.

Johnny Miller

"You're going to have to slow down, read books, pay attention to your stamp collection, and have interesting conversations with your wife."

The minister teed off on the ninth hole and promptly drove the ball into the middle of a sand trap. He hadn't missed a sand trap all day, and it was just too much for him. He took his driver and broke it over his knee. Then he grabbed his golf bag and pitched it into the middle of the lake. Next he scooped up his golf ball and threw it after the bag. Finally, through clenched teeth, he uttered his first words. "I'm gonna give it up," he muttered.

"Golf?" the caddy queried.

"No. The ministry."

Gilpin, a young minister, had just finished a round of golf with Charlton, a parishioner in his seventies. The minister was in a foul mood, having just been trounced by a man twice his age.

"Cheer up," said Charlton. "It's just a game. Why, you'll win in the end. You'll probably be burying me one of these days."

Gilpin shook his head. "Even then it'll be your hole."

Two women golfers were driving a cart to where their first drives had landed.

"Since I've been taking lessons, my drives have really straightened out," said the first. "Now I'm consistently shooting this course in under two gallons of gas."

Bob returned home after a round of golf and was greeted by his two young children.

"Did you win, Daddy? Did you win?"

Bob lifted the two up. "Kids, in golf it doesn't really matter if you win or lose. But your father got to hit the ball more than anyone else."

Finch was paired with a new member named Thornton, and it quickly became apparent that Thornton was not only new to the club, but new to golf. By the end of the front nine, Thornton had dug up more divots than the groundskeepers could hope to replace. He loudly cursed every other shot, and several times he flung clubs that narrowly missed Finch and his caddy. On the tenth tee, Finch drove down the middle, while Thornton's drive landed behind a large oak tree.

Surveying his ball, the duffer yelled over to Finch. "What club should I try?"

Finch smiled hopefully. "One in Cleveland?"

The reason they call it "golf" is that all the other four-letter words were used up.

Leslie Nielsen

McIntosh was an ardent golfer, and when he died and arrived at the Pearly Gates his first question to St. Peter was, "Where's the golf course?"

"Alas, Mr. McIntosh, I'm afraid we have no golf courses here," replied St. Peter.

Crestfallen, McIntosh walked to the side of the entrance to absorb the bad news. Then he heard a "pssst" and was startled to see the Devil standing near an elevator. The Devil looked around and then whispered, "McIntosh, we've got a seventy-two-hole championship course in Hell that's finer than anything you've ever played. Want to see?"

McIntosh nodded his assent and stepped into the elevator. A second later they arrived, and the doors opened.

"There it is," said the Devil, pointing to a magnificent verdant fairway stretching off to a bunkered first green next to a gorgeous lake. McIntosh entered the clubhouse, where he was handed a set of graphite clubs, clothes that fit perfectly, shoes, and a handtooled leather golf bag. Minutes later, he and the Devil were on the first tee.

"Wait a minute. Where are the woods?" asked McIntosh looking in his bag.

"No woods," smiled the Devil, handing him a 1-iron. "That's why they call it Hell."

If you break 100, watch your golf. If you break 80, watch your business.

Joey Adams

Ralph and Stephen were on the third tee, and Stephen was just about to hit, when a hearse followed by a caravan of cars went by on the road. Stephen glanced up, stopped his swing, took off his golf cap, and stood in silence until the procession had passed by. Ben, impressed with his friend's act of respect, said, "That was a very nice thing to do, Stephen."

Stephen teed his ball up again, swung through, and then spoke. "Nah. It was the least I could do. After all, we were married twenty-eight years next month."

A minister awoke early one beautiful Sunday morning in June. The birds were singing, the sun was shining, and he had an irresistible urge to take off for the golf course.

"Just this once couldn't hurt," he justified to himself as he phoned the assistant pastor to ask him to fill in. Then he threw his clubs in the trunk of his car and headed for the course.

It was early, and no one was about, not even the golf pro. As the pastor teed up his ball, he was very pleased with himself, thinking that no one had spotted him. But someone had.

"Look at that pastor down there!" said St. Peter to God. "I can't believe it, he's playing golf instead of performing his religious duties."

With that, the pastor uncorked the drive of his life some 350 yards down the middle of the fairway. The ball skimmed a rock, took two long bounces, rolled on the green and dropped into the hole.

"My goodness!" muttered an astonished St. Peter, observing the shot. He then turned to God. "I can't believe you let him get a hole in one."

God beamed an all-knowing smile. "Who's he going to tell?"

Robin was playing in the finals of the club tournament and had finished the front nine when his caddy developed a case of the hiccups. The constant hiccuping threw Robin off his game, and on the last hole he drove his tee shot deep into the woods. He threw his driver at the caddy and snarled, "That was due to you and your damn hiccups!"

"But I didn't hiccup then, Mr. Leech," the caddy pleaded.

"I know you didn't," barked Robin. "But I had allowed for it!"

"Fore"

The duffer flailed away at a ball imbedded in a sand trap. On the sixth swing he finally lofted the ball up, and it settled onto the green.

"Golf sure is a funny game," sighed the duffer as the caddy handed him his putter.

"It's not meant to be," replied the caddy.

If a lot of people gripped a knife and fork like they do a golf club, they'd starve to death.

Sam Snead

"McCord is such a thief," said Davis, "I'm afraid he's going to steal this new golf ball of mine."

Lydon looked over. "I wouldn't putt it past him."

You can talk to a fade, but a hook won't listen.

Lee Trevino

The foursome was on the third green when a limousine drove up on the road running alongside the hole. A window rolled down and a young woman dressed all in white and holding a bouquet leaned out the window.

"Bobby, Bobby," she sobbed. "You promised you'd meet me at the church."

"Not now, Tiffany," said Bobby, eyeing his putt. "I said if it rained."

If you think it's hard to meet new people, pick up the wrong ball.

Blake Lochrie

Rabbi Binswanger and Monsignor Burke played golf together every Wednesday. The two men of the cloth were on the fourth green, and the priest was eyeing his putt. He made the sign of the cross, swung through, and his putt rolled true and into the cup.

"Do you think that if I bless myself, Monsignor, I'll make my putt?" asked the rabbi.

"Not a chance," replied the monsignor.

"Why not?" inquired the rabbi.

"Because you're a terrible putter."

The new member was playing his first round of golf and was doing about as well as expected. After three hours in the sun, he and his exhausted caddy finally reached the eighteenth hole and finished the round.

"You must be really tired carrying those clubs," remarked the golfer to the caddy.

"I'm not tired from carrying the bag, sir," replied the caddy. "It's from counting the strokes!"

I had a wonderful experience on the golf course today. I had a hole in nothing. Missed the ball and sank the divot.

Don Adams

Sharon and Jackie were having a gin and tonic together after a round of golf.

"My husband has laid down the law," said Sharon. "He said, 'Make up your mind: it's either me or golf.'"

Sharon took a swallow of her drink and lamented, "I'm sure going to miss him."

Boswell and Hoffman had been playing golf together for years. The two were evenly matched until one spring Boswell's game suddenly improved and he began to beat Hoffman soundly every time they played. Hoffman went to the club pro for instruction, he bought new clubs, he changed his stance, but nothing seemed to help. Then he got an idea.

Hoffman went to his local bookstore and picked out three golf instruction books. He had them gift wrapped and instructed the clerk to mail them to Boswell. A week later Boswell's game had deteriorated to the point that the two were again evenly matched.

I play in the low 80s. If it's any hotter than that, I won't play.

Joe E. Brown

Duffer to scratch golfer: "Now tell me if you see me doing anything right!"

Two young men, Kevin and Pete, decided to take up golf and scheduled a lesson together with an instructor. After the lesson, they made a golf date for the following Thursday. When they got on the first tee, Pete pulled out a driver, checked off all the points the pro had told him, and promptly shanked a drive about forty yards out. Kevin also shanked his drive, but the shot glanced off a tree and hit a rock, which sent the ball flying toward the green. There it rolled up about ten feet from the pin. Pete glared at Kevin and snarled, "Why didn't you tell me you had been practicing!"

The American duffer had cursed and hacked his way around the ancient and venerable Scottish golf course, flinging away any club with which he happened to make a bad shot. Through it all the old caddy had uttered nary a word. Finally, the American flubbed an 8-iron shot and then hurled the offending club over a cliff, watching it till the club bounced on the rocks far below.

After a moment, the old Scotsman cleared his throat. "About your sweater, sir, will you be wanting that?"

Lee Trevino, on where professional golf would be without the sponsors' money:

I'll tell you where it would be. Julius Boros would be a bookkeeper in Connecticut; Arnold Palmer would still be in the Coast Guard; and I'd be back in Texas picking cotton."

"Your husband seems to have developed a new stance," observed one club member, pointing to the golfer on the first tee.

"Oh, that's not a new stance," replied the other. "That's a new husband."

Don Monroe finally convinced his business partner, Frank, that he ought to take up golf, using the argument that the exercise would be good for him. Reluctantly, Frank agreed and arrived at the club with a borrowed set of clubs. On the first tee, Frank took a mighty swing and somehow connected,driving the ball down the middle of the fairway. The ball took three or four bounces, hit the edge of the green and rolled into the cup.

"How do you like that," said Frank disgustedly. "I come out here for the exercise and I get a hole in one."

I learned English from American pros. That's why I speak so bad. I call it PGA English.

Roberto de Vicenzo

Reverend Johnson, entered in the club golf tournament, groaned when he saw that he was paired with the club duffer, a man who also drank and swore to excess. Lifting his eyes to Heaven in silent prayer, he headed for the first tee to meet Karraker, his partner.

Karraker hit first. After teeing up his ball, he dug his heels in, took a mighty swing, and missed.

"Goddam, I missed!" he yelled out when he realized the ball was still on the tee.

"Please, my good man, the Lord is listening," grimaced the minister.

Again Karraker addressed the ball and took a big swing, this time missing the tee by six inches.

"Goddam, I missed," he cried out.

"I implore you, Karraker, watch your language, the Lord hears you and might take vengeance," replied the minister.

Karraker dug his heels in, turned his body, cocked the club, and swung.

"Goddam, I missed!" snarled Karraker again.

With that the heavens grew dark, and clouds gathered and then parted. A mighty bolt of lightning shot down from the clouds and struck the minister where he stood.

"GODDAM, I MISSED!" thundered a Voice.

"You care more for golf than you do for me," sobbed Marilyn. "Why, you don't even remember what day we got married!"

"Sure I do," said Sid. "It was the day I sank that fifty-foot putt."

The two women were watching a golfer stuck in a sand trap on the eighteenth hole. Finally, the first woman turned to the other and said, "Whatever it is must be dead—he's stopped beating it."

Harry eyed his putt, took his stroke, and watched the ball drop in for a par. "That's a three," he sighed to Bert, who was keeping score.

"Why so glum, Harry? If I get a par I'm delighted."

Harry nodded. "Yeah, usually I am too. But ten years ago I got a hole in one right here. Once you've done that, anything less is terrible."

Bob walked over and put his putter back in his bag, then turned to his partner. "Isn't Fred out of the bunker yet? How many strokes has he had?"

His partner peered at Fred in the sand trap. "I'd say he's had about twelve strokes and one coronary."

"So, Maddy, is that new member any good at golf?" asked her friend Eddy.

"Absolutely. She's so good she doesn't have to cheat!"

I'm convinced the reason most people play golf is to wear clothes they would not otherwise be caught dead in.

Roger Simon

Brissie, a two-handicap golfer, stopped in a large sporting goods store and purchased a dozen golf balls.

"Shall I wrap them for you, sir?" the clerk asked.

"No, that's all right," Brissie replied. "I'll just drive them home."

The club pro walked over to two new members standing on the practice tee.

"Afternoon, ladies, and welcome to the club. Would either of you like to take a lesson?"

"Maybe my friend would," answered the first. "I learned yesterday."

Golf and sex are about the only two things you can enjoy without being very good at it.

Jimmy Demaret

Kate walked up to the club pro. "I've been playing golf for nearly a year. Can you give me some advice on how to lower my score?"

"Yeah. Just play the front nine."

At a cocktail party, Gutowsky, the well-known internist, was asked the secret of her success.

"It's easy," she replied. "When a patient comes in with stomach problems, I ask them if they play golf. If they say yes, I tell them to stop. If they say no, I tell them to start."

The two men had been behind a very slow twosome of women all morning, and they were getting increasingly annoyed at the slow pace. At the twelfth hole they hit to the green, and when they arrived, one woman was sitting on her cart while the other thrashed about in the deep rough.

"Don't you think you ought to go help your friend find her ball instead of relaxing on your cart?" snarled Fred at the woman.

"Oh, she's got her ball," said the woman sweetly. "She's looking for her club."

They say Sam Snead is a natural golfer. But if he didn't practice, he'd be a natural bad golfer.

Gary Player, on the
necessity of practice

"You know that partner I got paired with today?" asked Debbie. "He was so bad he even lost his ball in the washer."

Any game where a man sixty can beat a man thirty ain't no game.

Burt Shotton

Tom ran into his friend George on the train.

"George, I don't see you at the club anymore. Are you still playing golf?"

"No, I gave it up for bowling." his friend replied. "It's a lot cheaper. Why, last night I bowled for three hours and never lost a ball."

The middle-aged couple was finishing putting out when a ball whizzed by, narrowly missing them and landing behind the green. The wife was furious and stomped back to confront the golfer. "Listen, you old bag, that last shot of yours almost hit my husband."

"I'm very sorry," replied the woman, and then pointed at her partner. "Here, take a shot at mine."

If you watch a game, it's fun. If you play at it, it's recreation. If you work at it, it's golf.

Bob Hope

The two men were standing on the train platform in Chappaqua waiting for the arrival of the 8:14. "How's your daughter's golf game progressing, Mr. Sugar?" the first man asked.

Sugar shrugged. "She tells me she's going around in less and less each week."

"I have no doubts about that," said the first man. "But how's her golf?"

It's good sportsmanship not to pick up lost golf balls while they are still rolling.

Mark Twain

Harpootlian, at eighty-seven, was the oldest club member, but despite a hip replacement, near deafness, arthritis, and various other ailments, he still managed a round of golf each day. On one recent morning Harpootlian putted out on the ninth green, and as his caddy picked up his ball the boy said, "I'll put you down for a ten on that hole, Mr. Harpootlian."

"What's that, son? Speak up, please," said Harpootlian. "And make that a seven!"

You know the old rule: he who have fastest cart never have to play bad lie.

Mickey Mantle

"*I know 217 is a hellavu lot for nine holes, Lou, but I also think your caddie left a great deal to be desired.*"

Mike and Josh were having a beer in the clubhouse at the end of the day.

"How did your match go with Barnett?" asked Mike.

"He was incredible," Josh replied. "Booming his tee shots, hit the greens with every iron, every putt right on line."

"So I guess you lost," said Mike.

Josh beamed. "No, I won."

The duffer took a hard swing and topped another drive some two or three feet. Wiping his brow, he turned to the old caddy and said, "I suppose in your lifetime you've caddied for worse golfers."

The old caddy said nothing.

The golfer teed up another ball and then turned to the caddy. "I said, 'I suppose in your lifetime you've caddied for worse golfers.'"

"I heard what you said," the caddy responded. "I'm still thinking."

Bradley, the CEO of a large corporation, received a FAX stating that his wife had been kidnapped and was being held for ransom. "Bring $100,000 to the fourteenth hole of the Meadowwood Golf Course at noon. And no cops!"

High noon arrived, and Bradley was nowhere to been seen. It was nearly one o'clock when Bradley arrived with his clubs and a golf cart at the appointed tee. A masked man stepped out of the woods. "You were supposed to be here nearly an hour ago, Bradley. Where were you?"

"Hey, give me a break," said Bradley. "I've never played golf before."

The two matrons were just finishing their lunch when one asked, "Leslie, how come your sister, at her age, has taken up golf?"

"She read in the paper about a woman finding a diamond in the rough."

Golf: a young man's vice and an old man's penance.

Irvin S. Cobb

While at the club bar, Paul and Len got into an argument and decided to settle it by playing a round of golf. There was one problem: Paul shot in the 80s, while Len had never broken 100. Nevertheless, off the two went to play. Hours later Paul stomped into the bar and slumped on a stool. "Man, what's wrong with you, Paul?" asked the bartender. "Don't tell me you actually lost to that hacker?"

Paul nodded. "When we got to the first tee he asked for a handicap of two gotchas. And I agreed."

The bartender furrowed his brow. "What's a gotcha?"

Paul spread his hands. "Exactly. I said the same thing. Then when I got ready to hit my first shot, Len gooses me and yells 'gotcha!'

"I spent the next 18 holes wondering when the next gotcha was coming."

Sarah was talking to her friend Leslie. "I had problems with the grip when we were on vacation," said Sally.

"Oh, did you have to stay in bed?"

Bob was playing one of the country's historic course for the first time, and the caddy assigned to him was a grizzled, dour old veteran who had been hauling clubs for fifty years. For fifteen holes, the caddy kept up a running commentary about Bob's club choice, grip, stance, and strategy. On the sixteenth tee, Bob requested a 3-wood, only to hear the caddy's voice once again.

"I'd use a 4-iron on this one if I were you, sir."

Bob gritted his teeth, took the wood, and swung viciously at the ball. The long drive hooked to the left, bounced over a sand trap, and rolled up on the green some ten feet from the pin.

"What'd you think of that drive?" snarled Bob at the caddy.

"Well, sir, would've been a prettier shot with a 4-iron!"

While playing golf today I hit two good balls. I stepped on a rake.

Henny Youngman

The young honeymooners were out on the golf course, and the groom was explaining the basics of the sport to his bride.

"Tee the ball," he instructed.

"There's no need for baby talk," she huffed.

Jerry, a duffer, was talked into a round of golf by his neighbor Jay. On the first hole, Jerry teed up his ball, took a mighty swing, and whiffed. Addressing the ball again, he swung and again missed. A third and fourth swing were no better. Jerry flung his club down in disgust and stomped off to the clubhouse.

"You can't quit now," yelled Jay after him. "You've got a no-hitter going."

Two avid golfers were in prison for embezzlement. Undaunted by the fifteen years of confinement facing them, they continued to play golf each day without using clubs or balls.

"I had a five on the last hole. What you'd get?" said the first, writing down the number on an invisible scorecard.

"Had a four," replied the other.

"A four!" said the first incredulously. "I distinctly heard you take five swings."

"The first was a practice swing."

"It couldn't have been. I heard you grunt!"

"Gloria, I don't like the way you cheat keeping score," chided her partner.

"Really? What's your way?"

Tally, an obstetrician, and his friend James had been playing golf together for years. But now James, whose wife had just had a baby, was furious about a bill he had just received from Steve.

"Look at this," he yelled, and thrust the invoice into Tally's hand. "How can you charge $500 for the delivery room when you know as well as I do that Barbara delivered the baby on the front lawn of the hospital?"

"Okay," agreed Tally. Then he pulled out a pen, scratched out the words "Delivery Room Fee," and wrote in "Greens Fee."

Terry tried to restrain himself and keep his cursing down during the club tournament, especially since he was paired with a minister. But this day he had played a terrible front nine, lost two balls in the rough, and lost two more in the lake. With his last water shot, all control deserted him. He lifted his head and let go with sixty seconds of expletives. The minister was shocked speechless, but only for a moment. Then he felt obliged to respond.

"You know, don't you, Terry," he said in a calm voice, "that the best golfers in the world never resort to foul language."

Terry scowled. "I'm sure they don't. What the hell do they have to swear about?"

If you are going to throw a club, it is important to throw it ahead of you, down the fairway. That way you don't waste energy going back to pick it up.

Tommy Bolt

At the company's annual golf outing, Grimsley, the CEO, was talking to the marketing vice president. "I think that new assistant you hired is going to work out just fine, Peabody."

"I'm glad to hear that, Mr. Grimsley, but what makes you say it?"

"Well, he was in my foursome today, and on the third hole I shanked my drive, and it went into the woods. I then hit a 5-iron that landed in a sand trap about 150 yards from the green. That's when I knew your assistant would work out."

"Why, what happened?" asked Peabody.

"He conceded the putt."

The nattily dressed duffer, outfitted with expensive graphite clubs and a designer leather golf bag, was trying to engage the caddy in conversation. "So, my good man, how do you like my game so far?"

"I guess it's okay," replied the caddy, "but I still prefer golf."

A small-town judge was ready to tee off with two friends one afternoon when the new club pro asked if he could join them.

The three readily agreed, since it seemed like a good opportunity to get a free lesson. But instead of being helpful, the pro was openly critical of all of them, especially the judge's game. He pointed out flaws in the judge's shots, said his footwork was bad, his stance terrible, his club selection haphazard, and his swing a joke. This continued for the entire round, with the judge stoically bearing the brunt of the criticism.

When the judge finally putted out on the eighteenth hole, he breathed a sigh of relief that the long afternoon had ended. The foursome shook hands, and then the pro clapped the judge on the shoulder.

"Judge, thanks a lot. Remember, if you can't find anybody else to make a foursome, I'll be glad to play with you again.

The judge smiled thinly. "How about next Saturday?" he asked. "I don't think my friends here can make it, so why don't you invite your parents to play? Then after our round I can marry them."

"Thank you, God of Golf!"

"How was your golf game, dear?" asked Harvey's wife Jill.

"Well, I was hitting pretty well, but my eyesight's gotten so bad I couldn't see where the ball went."

"But you're seventy-five years old, Harvey!" admonished his wife. "Why don't you take my brother Pete along?"

"But he's eighty-five and doesn't even play golf anymore," protested Harvey.

"But he's got perfect eyesight. He could watch your ball," Jill pointed out.

The next day Harvey teed off with Pete looking on. Harvey swung, and the ball disappeared down the middle of the fairway. "Do you see it?" asked Harvey.

"Yup," Pete answered.

"Well, where is it?" yelled Harvey, peering off into the distance.

"I forget."

Never bet with anyone you meet on the first tee who has a deep suntan, a 1-iron in his bag, and squinty eyes.

Davey Marr

For four holes, Smedley kept up a continuous volley of statements trying to impress his golfing partner. He'd talk about his cars, his clothing budget, his impressive stock portfolio, his houses in the Caribbean and the

South of France. Gesturing toward his bag of clubs, he preened, "After I had those clubs custom-made at a cost of $10,000, I spent another $25,000 on private golf lessons."

"Really," breathed one of the golfers. "You should meet my cousin."

"Why? Is he a golfer?"

"No. He's a lawyer."

The two men were enjoying a drink at the nineteenth hole after playing nine holes. "You know, I used to play thirty-six holes a day," said the first.

His friend was impressed. "That's pretty good. What was your handicap?"

"My wife!"

Jasmine and Tiffany were relaxing after a round of golf and talking about their spouses. "I don't want to say that the romance has gone out of my marriage, Tiffany, but my sex drive is more like a putt."

The uglier a man's legs are, the better he plays golf. It's almost a law.

H. G. Wells

Barry was staying in a tiny hotel on a small Caribbean island and decided to play a round of golf at the local club course. He was assigned a caddy who carried the bag over one shoulder and a gun over the other. Barry, a little unsettled by seeing the rifle, hooked his first tee shot into the rough. When he went to take his second shot, an alligator charged him, but quick as a flash, the caddy shot the animal dead in his tracks.

"Weekdays, this is an easy par 3."

On the second tee, Barry again drove into the rough, where another alligator darted out to attack him. Once again, the caddy shot him in the nick of time.

On the third hole, Barry's iron shot from the fairway rolled into some mud right next to a sleeping alligator.

Barry looked expectantly at his caddy, who made no move to unshoulder the rifle. "Aren't you going to take care of the alligator?" asked Barry.

The caddy shook his head. "No extra shots on a par 3."

The golfer was trying to impress his guest with how rich and exclusive his country club was. "You know, the pro here makes more than the President of the United States."

"I'm not surprised," the guest responded. "He plays a better game."

The congressman was teeing up his ball when he stopped and turned to his partner. "Do you know why golf is like taxes?"

"No."

"You drive hard to get to the green, and then you end up in the hole."

There's an old saying: if a man comes home with sand in his cuffs and cockleburrs in his pants, don't ask him what he shot.

Sam Snead

"All the golfers think I'm a great doctor,
and all the doctors think I'm a great golfer."

The rain had been pouring down all day, but Ernie and Dave were undeterred. It was Wednesday, and that was the day they played golf. Ernie followed Dave and putted out, his shot raising a small rooster tail as it headed for the hole. Picking up his ball, Ernie looked up and then remarked to Dave, "Don't you just know that even with this lousy weather, Alice will want me to run errands."

The two golfers had just finished putting when all of a sudden it started to rain buckets. Quickly they took shelter under a giant oak tree in back of the green.

"What you'd get on that last hole?" said the golfer holding the scorecard.

"Five."

Just then a huge bolt of lightning crashed near the tree.

"Ah, better change that to seven."

"Foster, your game is getting to be an obsession," said Roberts disapprovingly. "It's starting to affect your business."

"But, boss," protested Foster. "my doctor said I should take my iron every day."

Golf appeals to the idiot in us and the child. Just how childlike golfers become is proven by their frequent inability to count past five.

John Updike

Give me my golf clubs, fresh air, a beautiful partner, and you can keep the golf clubs and the fresh air.

Jack Benny

It was a beautiful autumn day, and Ferris was enjoying a round of golf at his club. Flubbing a 3-wood, he watched the ball dribble into the woods on the left just as a pheasant hunter emerged from the same spot.

"Hey, you," yelled Ferris. "There are no hunters allowed here. This is strictly for golfers."

The hunter put his finger to his lips. "If you don't tell on me, I won't tell on you."

Prayer never seems to work for me on the golf course. I think it has something to do with my being a terrible putter.

Reverend Billy Graham

"Look, I'm as sorry about Lou's heart attack as you are, but that ball is not a gimme."

As they had been doing since the invention of the golf ball, Jesus and Moses were enjoying the Heavenly weather by playing a weekly round of golf. At the third hole, Jesus hit a perfect drive that bounced up in front of a small lake with the green sitting on the other side. Sitting on the edge of the far shore was the pin. "You've got your work cut out for you here," Moses offered, surveying the green in the distance. "I think you'll need a 5-iron for this shot."

Jesus stroked his chin and then selected a club. "I don't think so. The other day I was watching Jack Nicklaus on television, and he was faced with this very same shot. And he used a 7-iron." With that, he hit a perfect shot that drove high in the air and plunked down in the lake short of the green. Moses shook his head, walked on up to the lake, parted the waters and retrieved the ball.

"I told you," he said, as he hand the ball to Jesus. "A 5-iron."

Jesus ignored his companion and placed the ball on the ground. Swinging harder this time, he sent the 7-iron shot toward the green. Once again, it plopped in the lake. Moses hiked up his robes and rescued the ball. Three more times the scene was repeated until Moses refused to retrieve the ball. Jesus shrugged and strolled across the water to fish for his ball.

Just then, another golfer who had been observing for five minutes walked up to Moses. Gesturing to Jesus returning with his ball, he said, "That guy taking all the swings. Who does he think he is? God?"

Moses shook his head. "No. He thinks he's Jack Nicklaus."

A duffer had been whacking his way around eighteen holes, making the course twice as long for himself and his exhausted caddy. Coming up to the eighteenth hole, the caddy handed the man a 7-iron and stepped back. The golfer took a wild swing and lofted a large divot about five yards. The ball progressed a few yards further. The golfer walked over and picked up the divot. Turning to his caddy he asked, "What should I do with this?"

"I'd suggest you take it home to practice on!"

Thompson, an eight-handicap golfer, finished his first week of vacation with yet another terrible round. He was so despondent and disheartened by his miserable play that he went into the locker room, walked into the shower area, took out a razor and, standing over the washbasin, slashed his wrists. As he stood there watching the blood gush into the sink, a friend walked into the locker room and spotted Thompson. "Hey, you want to play a round tomorrow?"

Thompson immediately clamped his wrists together and looked up. "What time?"

Freddie was unloading her clubs from the trunk of her car, when her friend walked by. "Mandy!" Freddie yelled. "I am so excited about being in this tournament that I had my ball retriever regripped!"

A young priest was playing alone when he approached the fifth tee and looked out at the far green. Between him and the green was a small lake. As he was pondering which club to use, a Heavenly voice spoke up. "Use a 7-iron."

The young priest was open-mouthed at this divine intervention and did as he was bid.

"Now put down a new ball."

Again, the priest did as he was told.

"Now take a practice swing," the voice directed. The priest took a swing, and the voice spoke again.

"Put down an old ball."

Jock and Angus had just finished eighteen holes of golf and hurried into the club bar for a glass of scotch. Drinks were served, and the two settled into chairs. They scraped the ice out of their beards and gazed out the window, where the sea was being churned up by the thirty-mile-per hour wind.

"So Jock," Angus finally said. "Same time next week?"

"Aye, Angus," Jock replied. "Weather permitting."

On this particular Saturday morning, Jeffrey was playing a round of golf by himself when all of a sudden the ghost of his old business partner appeared before him. "Ben, is that you?" the astonished Jeffrey asked.

"Yes, Jeffrey, it's me, your old partner. I've been in Heaven since I died two years ago."

"Gosh, Ben. What's it like up there?"

"Well, there are some good things and some bad things about Heaven. The golf courses are magnificent. Rolling fairways, lush greens, beautiful clubhouses, and you never have to wait."

Jeffrey scratched his head. "All that sounds great. What could possibly be bad about it?"

The ghost looked at Jeffrey. "You and I have a tee time of 8:00 tomorrow."

Gimme: an agreement between two losers who can't putt.

Jim Bishop

Joanna and Sylvia were unloading their clubs from the trunk of the car, when Sylvia noticed her friend stuffing a paper bag in the her pocket. "What've you got there?" she asked. "Something to help your game?"

"Yes," Joanna replied. "it'll help me get more birdies and eagles."

"What is it?"

"Birdseed!"

Cliff had been marooned on a desert island for three years. He was sitting on the sand staring at the ocean when all of a sudden a scuba diver rose up out of the surf. Not only was it the first human he'd encountered in four years, as the diver got closer Cliff saw that she was the most gorgeous woman he'd ever seen.

Walking up on shore, she looked down at Cliff, reached into her wet suit, and produced a cigarette and matches."This is fantastic. I must be dreaming," said Cliff, lighting up and taking a long drag.

The diver then put her hand in the wet suit and pulled out a plastic cup and gave it to him. Taking a sip, he marveled, "A vodka martini. And with two olives."

"You would think that up here, on the last hole, they would let you keep the ball."

The diver then unzipped her wet suit a few inches and looked down at Cliff. "Are you ready to play around?" she breathed sexily.

Cliff gaped at the diver. "Don't tell me you've got golf clubs in there!"

Isn't it fun to go out on the course and lie in the sun?

Bob Hope

"Say, Keith, did you hear about Fred trying to drown himself in the lake on the tenth hole?"

"That's terrible. What happened?"

"Nothing. He couldn't keep his head down there either."

Hook: the addiction of 50 percent of all golfers.
Slice: the weakness of the other half.

Jim Bishop